VEGETARIAN DIABETIC RENAL DIET COOKBOOK

Teresa Ballard

© 2024 by Teresa Ballard

All rights reserved. No part of this book may be reproduced, stored in a retrieval system, or transmitted in any form or by any means, electronic, mechanical, photocopying, recording, or otherwise, without the prior written permission of the publisher, except for brief quotations in critical reviews or article

Disclaimer:

The information provided in this book is for general informational purposes only. While every effort has been made to ensure that the content is accurate and up-to-date, the author and the publisher make no representations or warranties of any kind, express or implied, about the completeness, accuracy, reliability, suitability, or availability of the information contained within these pages. Any reliance you place on such information is strictly at your own risk.

OTHER BOOKS BY THE AUTHOR

Low Potassium Slow Cooker Cookbook

Low Potassium Instant Pot Cookbook

Low Potassium Air Fryer Cookbook

Low Potassium Cookbook for Seniors

Vegetarian Low potassium Cookbook

Vegan Low Potassium Cookbook

Low Sodium Slow Cooker cookbook

Low Sodium Instant Pot Cookbook

Low Sodium Air Fryer Cookbook

Low Sodium Cookbook for Congestive Heart Failure

Low Sodium Cookbook for Kidney Disease

Low Sodium Cookbook for Beginners

Vegetarian Low Sodium Cookbook

Vegan Low Sodium Cookbook

Low Sodium Cookbook for Seniors

Low Potassium cookbook for Beginners

SCAN THE QR CODE BELOW TO SEE MORE BOOKS BY THE AUTHOR

TABLE OF CONTENTS

INTRODUCTION 1

CHAPTER ONE: Understanding Diabetes and Renal Health 5

    What is Diabetes? 5

    What is Renal Disease? 6

    Managing Diabetes and Renal Health Together 6

CHAPTER TWO: Basics of a Vegetarian Diet for Diabetes and Renal Health 9

    Benefits of a Vegetarian Diet: 9

    Nutritional Considerations: 11

CHAPTER THREE: Breakfast Recipes 13

    1. Quinoa Breakfast Bowl 13

    2. Vegetable Omelet 14

    3. Spinach and Feta Breakfast Wrap 15

    4. Greek Yogurt Parfait 16

    5. Avocado Toast with Poached Egg 17

    6. Chia Seed Pudding 18

    7. Tofu Scramble 19

    8. Banana Walnut Muffins 20

    9. Zucchini Pancakes 22

    10. Sweet Potato Breakfast Bowl 24

CHAPTER FOUR: Lunch Recipes 25

    11. Quinoa and Black Bean Salad 25

    12. Vegetable Stir-Fry 27

    13. Lentil Soup 28

    14. Chickpea Salad Wraps 30

    15. Vegetarian Chili 32

    16. Mediterranean Quinoa Salad 34

    17. Eggplant and Tomato Pasta 36

    18. Spinach and Chickpea Curry 38

    19. Stuffed Bell Peppers 39

    20. Vegetable and Lentil Curry 40

CHAPTER FIVE: Dinner Recipes 43

    21. Grilled Portobello Mushroom Steaks 43

    22. Vegetable Stir-Fry with Tofu 45

    23. Spaghetti Squash with Marinara Sauce 47

    24. Black Bean and Sweet Potato Tacos 49

    25. Mushroom and Spinach Risotto 51

    26. Stuffed Bell Peppers with Quinoa and Black Beans 53

    27. Vegetarian Lentil Shepherd's Pie 55

    28. Eggplant Parmesan 57

    29. Vegetarian Chili 59

    30. Mediterranean Stuffed Peppers 61

CHAPTER SIX: Snacks and Appetizers 63

    31. Hummus with Vegetable Sticks 63

    32. Guacamole with Whole Wheat Pita Chips 65

    33. Cucumber and Tomato Salad 66

    34. Greek Yogurt Dip with Sliced Bell Peppers 67

    35. Roasted Chickpeas 68

    36. Stuffed Cherry Tomatoes 70

    37. Spinach and Feta Phyllo Triangles 71

    38. Cucumber Roll-Ups 73

    39. Stuffed Mushrooms 74

    40. Edamame Salad 76

CHAPTER SEVEN: Desserts 77

    41. Banana Oatmeal Cookies 77

    42. Greek Yogurt Parfait with Berries 78

    43. Baked Apples with Cinnamon 79

    44. Chia Seed Pudding 80

    45. Frozen Banana Bites 81

    46. Coconut Rice Pudding 82

    47. Berry Sorbet 83

    48. Chocolate Avocado Mousse 84

    49. Fruit Salad with Mint-Lime Dressing 85

    50. Baked Pears with Cinnamon 86

CHAPTER EIGHT: Beverages 87

    51.   Cucumber Mint Cooler 87

    52.   Berry Blast Smoothie 88

    53.   Watermelon Lime Refresher 89

    54.   Green Tea Lemonade 90

    55.   Pineapple Ginger Punch 91

    56.   Coconut Watermelon Cooler 92

    57.   Cranberry Orange Spritzer 93

    58.   Minty Lime Iced Tea 94

    59.   Peach Basil Sparkler 95

    60.   Tropical Green Smoothie 96

CONCLUSION 97

BONUS:30 DAY MEAL PLAN 99

INTRODUCTION

In the quiet halls of a bustling hospital, amidst the constant hum of machines and the hurried footsteps of healthcare professionals, there exists a world often overlooked yet profoundly impactful—the world of nutrition. It is here, in the delicate balance between sustenance and health, that lives are transformed, where the whisper of a meal plan can hold the power to rewrite destinies. This is a story of one such transformation, a tale of resilience, hope, and the remarkable fusion of culinary art and medical science—a story that begins with Mrs. Carol.

Picture a serene hospital room adorned with the gentle glow of morning sunlight filtering through translucent curtains. In the midst of this tranquility sits Mrs. Carol, a woman whose weary eyes mirrored the weight of her medical diagnosis. Her journey with diabetes and renal complications had been fraught with challenges, each meal becoming a minefield of dietary restrictions and health concerns. As an experienced nutritionist, I had encountered countless individuals like Mrs. Carol, each grappling with their own unique battles against chronic illness. Yet, it was in her quiet determination and unwavering spirit that I found inspiration to embark on a journey of innovation—a journey that would lead to the creation of the Vegetarian Diabetic Renal Diet Cookbook.

Our initial conversations were tentative, filled with the apprehension that often accompanies the unknown. Mrs. Carol spoke of her frustrations, her fears, and the overwhelming sense of isolation that permeated her dietary choices.

She longed for a solution—a lifeline that would not only nourish her body but also feed her soul. It was in these moments of vulnerability that the seeds of collaboration were sown, as we embarked on a quest to redefine the boundaries of diabetic and renal-friendly cuisine.

The journey was not without its challenges. We navigated through the labyrinth of nutritional guidelines, meticulously crafting recipes that balanced flavor with functionality, indulgence with intentionality. Each dish became a canvas upon which we painted a symphony of colors, textures, and aromas—a culinary masterpiece designed to tantalize the taste buds and heal the body from within.

As the weeks passed, Mrs. Carol's transformation unfolded before my eyes, a testament to the power of food as medicine. Her once weary countenance was replaced by a radiant glow, her energy levels soared, and her zest for life reignited with newfound vigor. With each passing day, she embraced the cookbook with fervor, finding solace in its pages and empowerment in its recipes. It became more than just a collection of dishes—it was a lifeline, a companion on her journey to reclaiming her health and rediscovering the joys of nourishment.

Yet, Mrs. Carol's story is but a single thread in the rich tapestry of human experience—a reminder that behind every diagnosis lies a story waiting to be told, a life waiting to be transformed. It is my hope that within the pages of this cookbook, you will find not only recipes to nourish the body but also stories to nourish the soul. From the comforting embrace of a hearty soup to the decadent delight of a guilt-free dessert, each dish is infused with the love, passion, and dedication that fueled its creation.

I invite you to embark on a journey of culinary exploration—a journey that transcends the boundaries of tradition and defies the limitations of chronic illness. Within these pages, you will find more than just recipes—you will find hope, inspiration, and the promise of a brighter tomorrow. For in the kitchen, as in life, the power to heal lies not in the ingredients alone, but in the love and care with which they are prepared. Welcome to the Vegetarian Diabetic Renal Diet Cookbook—a celebration of health, happiness, and the infinite possibilities that lie within each delicious bite.

4 VEGETARIAN DIABETIC RENAL DIET COOKBOOK

CHAPTER ONE: Understanding Diabetes and Renal Health

Welcome to the journey of understanding the intricate relationship between diabetes and renal health. In this chapter, we will delve into the depths of these two conditions, exploring what they are, how they intertwine, and most importantly, how you can manage them effectively while embracing a vegetarian lifestyle. So, let's embark on this enlightening journey together.

What is Diabetes?

Imagine your body as a finely tuned machine, where each part plays a crucial role in maintaining balance and harmony. Diabetes, unfortunately, disrupts this delicate equilibrium. At its core, diabetes is a chronic condition characterized by elevated levels of glucose (sugar) in the blood. This elevation occurs either because the body doesn't produce enough insulin (Type 1 diabetes) or because the cells become resistant to insulin's effects (Type 2 diabetes).

When you consume food, your body breaks down carbohydrates into glucose, which serves as the primary source of energy. Insulin, a hormone produced by the pancreas, acts as the key that unlocks cells, allowing glucose to enter and fuel your body. In diabetes, this process falters, leading to a buildup of glucose in the bloodstream.

The consequences of uncontrolled diabetes are far-reaching, affecting various organs and systems in your body. From cardiovascular complications to nerve damage, the repercussions of high blood sugar levels are profound. Moreover, diabetes is a silent predator, often progressing stealthily until complications arise.

What is Renal Disease?

Now, let's shift our focus to another critical player in this narrative: renal disease. Your kidneys, those bean-shaped organs nestled snugly in your lower back, play a vital role in maintaining overall health. They act as the body's filtration system, removing waste products and excess fluids from the blood through urine.

Renal disease, also known as kidney disease, encompasses a spectrum of conditions that impair kidney function. Chronic kidney disease (CKD), in particular, is a progressive condition characterized by gradual loss of kidney function over time. Diabetes is one of the leading causes of CKD, further emphasizing the intricate connection between these two conditions.

As CKD progresses, the kidneys become less efficient at filtering waste and regulating fluid balance, leading to a buildup of toxins and fluid in the body. Left unchecked, CKD can culminate in end-stage renal disease (ESRD), where the kidneys lose their ability to function altogether, necessitating dialysis or kidney transplantation for survival.

Managing Diabetes and Renal Health Together

Now that we've gained a deeper understanding of diabetes and renal health, the question arises: how can you manage these two conditions simultaneously? The key lies in adopting a holistic approach that addresses both the dietary and lifestyle factors contributing to their progression.

Mindful Eating: As a vegetarian diabetic with renal concerns, your dietary choices play a pivotal role in managing your health. Opt for whole, unprocessed foods that are rich in nutrients and low in sodium, phosphorus, and potassium.

Focus on incorporating a variety of fruits, vegetables, whole grains, and plant-based proteins into your meals while keeping a close eye on portion sizes and carbohydrate intake.

Blood Sugar Monitoring: Regular monitoring of your blood sugar levels is essential for keeping your diabetes in check. Work closely with your healthcare provider to establish target ranges and develop a personalized monitoring plan. By staying vigilant and proactive, you can prevent dangerous spikes or dips in blood sugar that may exacerbate renal complications.

Hydration: Adequate hydration is crucial for supporting kidney function and preventing dehydration, especially if you have CKD. Aim to drink plenty of water throughout the day, but be mindful of your fluid intake if you're on a fluid-restricted diet. Herbal teas, infused water, and low-sodium broths are excellent alternatives to plain water, adding flavor without compromising your renal health.

Physical Activity: Regular exercise offers a multitude of benefits for both diabetes and renal health. Engage in activities that you enjoy, such as walking, swimming, or yoga, aiming for at least 30 minutes of moderate-intensity exercise most days of the week. Exercise helps improve insulin sensitivity, lower blood pressure, and promote overall well-being, making it a cornerstone of your management plan.

Medication Adherence: If you're prescribed medications to manage your diabetes or CKD, it's imperative to take them as directed by your healthcare provider. Skipping doses or altering your medication regimen without medical supervision can have serious consequences, potentially compromising your health and exacerbating your condition.

CHAPTER TWO: Basics of a Vegetarian Diet for Diabetes and Renal Health

Welcome to Chapter Two of your Vegetarian Diabetic Renal Diet Cookbook journey! In this chapter, we delve into the fundamentals of a vegetarian diet tailored specifically for managing diabetes and promoting renal health. Whether you're new to the world of plant-based eating or looking to refine your existing approach, understanding the benefits and nutritional considerations of this dietary lifestyle is crucial. So, grab your favorite beverage, settle in, and let's explore the ins and outs of vegetarianism in the context of diabetes and renal wellness.

Benefits of a Vegetarian Diet:

Embracing a vegetarian diet can offer a myriad of benefits for both your diabetes management and renal health. Here's a closer look at why this dietary approach is worth considering:

Improved Blood Sugar Control: Plant-based diets, rich in fiber, complex carbohydrates, and nutrient-dense foods, have been shown to help stabilize blood sugar levels. By reducing the intake of processed foods and focusing on whole, natural ingredients, you can better manage your diabetes and potentially reduce the need for medication.

Lower Risk of Heart Disease: Diabetes and kidney disease often coincide with an increased risk of cardiovascular complications.

A vegetarian diet, particularly one that emphasizes fruits, vegetables, whole grains, and healthy fats, can significantly lower the risk of heart disease by reducing cholesterol levels, blood pressure, and inflammation.

Kidney-Friendly Nutrition: For individuals with renal issues, such as chronic kidney disease (CKD), a vegetarian diet can provide the necessary nutrients while minimizing the burden on the kidneys. By moderating protein intake and prioritizing plant-based sources of protein, you can help preserve kidney function and slow the progression of CKD.

Weight Management: Maintaining a healthy weight is essential for managing diabetes and reducing the risk of kidney complications. Vegetarian diets tend to be lower in calories and saturated fats while being rich in fiber and water content, promoting satiety and aiding weight loss or maintenance efforts.

Enhanced Nutrient Intake: A well-planned vegetarian diet can provide an abundance of essential nutrients, including vitamins, minerals, antioxidants, and phytonutrients. By incorporating a variety of colorful fruits, vegetables, whole grains, legumes, nuts, and seeds into your meals, you can ensure you're meeting your nutritional needs while supporting overall health.

Sustainable and Ethical: Beyond personal health benefits, adopting a vegetarian diet aligns with sustainable and ethical principles. By reducing reliance on animal products, you contribute to environmental conservation, animal welfare, and global food security, making a positive impact on both your health and the planet.

Nutritional Considerations:

While the benefits of a vegetarian diet are clear, it's essential to pay attention to the nutritional aspects to ensure you're meeting your specific dietary requirements, especially when managing diabetes and renal health. Here are some key considerations to keep in mind:

Balanced Macronutrients: A balanced vegetarian diet should include adequate amounts of carbohydrates, protein, and fats. Aim to incorporate a variety of plant-based sources of each macronutrient to ensure you're getting a diverse array of nutrients. For carbohydrates, focus on whole grains, fruits, and vegetables; for protein, include beans, lentils, tofu, tempeh, nuts, and seeds; and for fats, choose healthy sources like avocados, olive oil, and nuts.

Protein Moderation: While protein is essential for overall health, excessive protein intake can put strain on the kidneys, particularly for individuals with renal impairment. Aim for moderate protein consumption and choose plant-based sources whenever possible. Incorporate a variety of legumes, nuts, seeds, and soy products into your meals to meet your protein needs without overloading on animal-based proteins.

Mindful Carbohydrates: Carbohydrate management is crucial for blood sugar control in diabetes. Opt for complex carbohydrates with a low glycemic index, such as whole grains, legumes, and non-starchy vegetables, which are digested more slowly and have a gentler impact on blood glucose levels. Limit refined carbohydrates and sugary foods, which can cause spikes in blood sugar.

Fiber-Rich Foods: Fiber plays a key role in diabetes management by slowing down the absorption of sugar, promoting satiety, and supporting digestive health. Aim to include plenty of fiber-rich foods in your vegetarian diet, such as fruits, vegetables, whole grains, legumes, nuts, and seeds. Shoot for at least 25-30 grams of fiber per day to reap the full benefits.

Micronutrient Focus: Pay attention to micronutrients like vitamins and minerals, which are essential for overall health and wellbeing. Some nutrients of particular importance for individuals with diabetes and renal issues include potassium, magnesium, vitamin D, and B vitamins. Incorporate a variety of nutrient-dense foods into your meals to ensure you're getting a broad spectrum of vitamins and minerals.

Hydration: Proper hydration is essential for kidney health, particularly for individuals with renal impairment. Aim to drink plenty of water throughout the day to stay hydrated and support kidney function. Limit the intake of sugary beverages and opt for water, herbal teas, or infused water instead.

CHAPTER THREE: Breakfast Recipes

1. Quinoa Breakfast Bowl

Servings: 2

Cooking Time: 20 minutes

Ingredients:

1 cup cooked quinoa

1/2 cup sliced strawberries

1/4 cup chopped almonds

1 tablespoon honey

1/2 teaspoon cinnamon

Preparation Method:

In a bowl, combine cooked quinoa, sliced strawberries, and chopped almonds.

Drizzle honey over the top and sprinkle with cinnamon.

Mix well and serve.

Nutritional Info: Calories: 250 | Carbs: 35g | Protein: 6g | Fat: 10g | Potassium: 280mg | Sodium: 5mg | Cholesterol: 0mg

2. Vegetable Omelet

Servings: 1

Cooking Time: 15 minutes

Ingredients:

2 eggs

1/4 cup diced bell peppers

1/4 cup diced onions

1/4 cup diced tomatoes

1 tablespoon olive oil

Salt and pepper to taste

Preparation Method:

Heat olive oil in a non-stick pan over medium heat.

Sautee bell peppers, onions, and tomatoes until soft.

Beat eggs in a bowl, season with salt and pepper, and pour over the vegetables.

Cook until the omelet is set, then fold in half and serve.

Nutritional Info: Calories: 280 | Carbs: 9g | Protein: 14g | Fat: 20g | Potassium: 320mg | Sodium: 250mg | Cholesterol: 370mg

3. Spinach and Feta Breakfast Wrap

Servings: 2

Cooking Time: 10 minutes

Ingredients:

2 whole wheat tortillas

1 cup fresh spinach

1/4 cup crumbled feta cheese

2 eggs, scrambled

Salt and pepper to taste

Preparation Method:

Warm the tortillas in a skillet or microwave.

Layer spinach, scrambled eggs, and feta cheese on each tortilla.

Season with salt and pepper, then roll up the tortillas.

Serve immediately.

Nutritional Info: Calories: 310 | Carbs: 25g | Protein: 17g | Fat: 16g | Potassium: 380mg | Sodium: 620mg | Cholesterol: 220mg

4. Greek Yogurt Parfait

Servings: 1

Cooking Time: 5 minutes

Ingredients:

1/2 cup plain Greek yogurt

1/4 cup diced mixed berries (strawberries, blueberries, raspberries)

2 tablespoons chopped walnuts

1 tablespoon honey

Preparation Method:

In a glass, layer Greek yogurt, mixed berries, and chopped walnuts.

Drizzle honey over the top.

Repeat layers if desired.

Serve immediately.

Nutritional Info: Calories: 250 | Carbs: 20g | Protein: 12g | Fat: 14g | Potassium: 280mg | Sodium: 70mg | Cholesterol: 10mg

5. Avocado Toast with Poached Egg

Servings: 1

Cooking Time: 10 minutes

Ingredients:

1 slice whole wheat bread, toasted

1/2 avocado, mashed

1 egg

Salt and pepper to taste

Preparation Method:

Poach the egg to desired doneness.

Spread mashed avocado on toasted bread.

Place the poached egg on top.

Season with salt and pepper.

Serve immediately.

Nutritional Info: Calories: 260 | Carbs: 20g | Protein: 12g | Fat: 15g | Potassium: 400mg | Sodium: 200mg | Cholesterol: 185mg

6. Chia Seed Pudding

Servings: 2

Preparation Time: 5 minutes (plus overnight chilling)

Ingredients:

1/4 cup chia seeds

1 cup unsweetened almond milk

1 tablespoon honey

1/2 teaspoon vanilla extract

Fresh berries for topping

Preparation Method:

In a bowl, mix chia seeds, almond milk, honey, and vanilla extract.

Cover and refrigerate overnight or for at least 4 hours until thickened.

Serve topped with fresh berries.

Nutritional Info: Calories: 150 | Carbs: 15g | Protein: 5g | Fat: 8g | Potassium: 180mg | Sodium: 80mg | Cholesterol: 0mg

7. Tofu Scramble

Servings: 2

Cooking Time: 15 minutes

Ingredients:

1 tablespoon olive oil

1/2 block extra-firm tofu, crumbled

1/4 cup diced bell peppers

1/4 cup diced onions

1/4 cup diced tomatoes

1/2 teaspoon turmeric

Salt and pepper to taste

Preparation Method:

Heat olive oil in a skillet over medium heat.

Add tofu, bell peppers, onions, and tomatoes.

Sprinkle with turmeric, salt, and pepper.

Cook until vegetables are tender and tofu is heated through.

Serve hot.

Nutritional Info: Calories: 200 | Carbs: 10g | Protein: 15g | Fat: 12g | Potassium: 320mg | Sodium: 10mg | Cholesterol: 0mg

8. Banana Walnut Muffins

Servings: 12

Cooking Time: 25 minutes

Ingredients:

2 ripe bananas, mashed

1/4 cup unsweetened applesauce

1/4 cup honey

1/4 cup olive oil

2 eggs

1 teaspoon vanilla extract

1 1/2 cups whole wheat flour

1 teaspoon baking soda

1/2 teaspoon cinnamon

1/4 teaspoon salt

1/2 cup chopped walnuts

Preparation Method:

Preheat oven to 350°F (175°C) and line a muffin tin with liners.

In a large bowl, mix mashed bananas, applesauce, honey, olive oil, eggs, and vanilla extract.

In another bowl, combine flour, baking soda, cinnamon, and salt.

Gradually add the dry ingredients to the wet ingredients, mixing until just combined.

Fold in chopped walnuts.

Divide the batter evenly among the muffin cups.

Bake for 20-25 minutes or until a toothpick inserted into the center comes out clean.

Let cool before serving.

Nutritional Info: Calories: 180 | Carbs: 25g | Protein: 4g | Fat: 8g | Potassium: 180mg | Sodium: 150mg | Cholesterol: 30mg

9. Zucchini Pancakes

Servings: 4

Cooking Time: 20 minutes

Ingredients:

2 cups grated zucchini

1/2 cup whole wheat flour

2 eggs

1/4 cup chopped fresh parsley

1/4 cup grated Parmesan cheese

1/2 teaspoon baking powder

Salt and pepper to taste

Olive oil for cooking

Preparation Method:

Place grated zucchini in a clean kitchen towel and squeeze out excess moisture.

In a large bowl, combine zucchini, whole wheat flour, eggs, parsley, Parmesan cheese, baking powder, salt, and pepper.

Heat olive oil in a skillet over medium heat.

Drop spoonfuls of batter onto the skillet and cook until golden brown on both sides, about 3-4 minutes per side.

Serve hot with your favorite sauce or yogurt.

Nutritional Info: Calories: 150 | Carbs: 12g | Protein: 8g | Fat: 7g | Potassium: 300mg | Sodium: 170mg | Cholesterol: 100mg

10. Sweet Potato Breakfast Bowl

Servings: 2

Cooking Time: 30 minutes

Ingredients:

1 large sweet potato, peeled and diced

1 tablespoon olive oil and 1/2 teaspoon paprika

1/2 teaspoon garlic powder

Salt and pepper to taste

1 cup cooked quinoa and 1/4 cup diced red bell pepper

1/4 cup diced green onions and 1/4 cup crumbled feta cheese

Preparation Method:

Preheat oven to 400°F (200°C).

Toss diced sweet potato with olive oil, paprika, garlic powder, salt, and pepper.

Spread sweet potatoes in a single layer on a baking sheet and roast for 20-25 minutes, until tender and slightly caramelized.

In a bowl, layer cooked quinoa, roasted sweet potatoes, diced red bell pepper, green onions, and crumbled feta cheese.

Serve warm.

Nutritional Info: Calories: 280 | Carbs: 35g | Protein: 8g | Fat: 12g | Potassium: 450mg | Sodium: 320mg | Cholesterol: 15mg

CHAPTER FOUR: Lunch Recipes

11. Quinoa and Black Bean Salad

Servings: 4

Cooking Time: 20 minutes

Ingredients:

1 cup quinoa, cooked

1 can (15 oz) black beans, drained and rinsed

1 cup diced tomatoes

1/2 cup diced bell peppers

1/4 cup chopped cilantro

2 tablespoons olive oil

1 tablespoon lime juice

Salt and pepper to taste

Preparation Method:

In a large bowl, combine cooked quinoa, black beans, tomatoes, bell peppers, and cilantro.

In a small bowl, whisk together olive oil, lime juice, salt, and pepper to make the dressing.

Pour the dressing over the salad and toss to combine.

Serve chilled or at room temperature.

Nutritional Info: Calories: 280 | Carbs: 40g | Protein: 10g | Fat: 9g | Potassium: 450mg | Sodium: 200mg | Cholesterol: 0mg

12. Vegetable Stir-Fry

Servings: 2

Cooking Time: 15 minutes

Ingredients:

2 cups mixed vegetables (such as bell peppers, broccoli, carrots, and snap peas)

1 tablespoon olive oil

2 cloves garlic, minced

1 tablespoon low-sodium soy sauce

1 teaspoon sesame oil

1/2 teaspoon ginger, grated

Cooked brown rice for serving

Preparation Method:

Heat olive oil in a large skillet or wok over medium-high heat.

Add minced garlic and grated ginger, cook for 1 minute until fragrant.

Add mixed vegetables and stir-fry for 5-7 minutes until tender-crisp.

Drizzle soy sauce and sesame oil over the vegetables, toss to coat evenly.

Serve hot over cooked brown rice.

Nutritional Info: Calories: 220 | Carbs: 30g | Protein: 6g | Fat: 9g | Potassium: 380mg | Sodium: 300mg | Cholesterol: 0mg

13. Lentil Soup

Servings: 6

Cooking Time: 30 minutes

Ingredients:

1 cup dried green lentils, rinsed

1 onion, diced

2 carrots, diced

2 stalks celery, diced

2 cloves garlic, minced

6 cups vegetable broth

1 teaspoon dried thyme

Salt and pepper to taste

Fresh parsley for garnish

Preparation Method:

In a large pot, sauté diced onion, carrots, celery, and garlic until softened.

Add dried lentils, vegetable broth, and dried thyme to the pot.

Bring to a boil, then reduce heat and simmer for 20-25 minutes until lentils are tender.

Season with salt and pepper to taste.

Garnish with fresh parsley before serving.

Nutritional Info: Calories: 180 | Carbs: 30g | Protein: 10g | Fat: 1g | Potassium: 550mg | Sodium: 690mg | Cholesterol: 0mg

14. Chickpea Salad Wraps

Servings: 4

Preparation Time: 15 minutes

Ingredients:

1 can (15 oz) chickpeas, drained and rinsed

1/4 cup diced red onion

1/4 cup diced cucumber

1/4 cup diced bell pepper

2 tablespoons chopped fresh parsley

2 tablespoons lemon juice

1 tablespoon olive oil

Salt and pepper to taste

4 whole wheat tortillas

Preparation Method:

In a bowl, mash the chickpeas with a fork or potato masher until chunky.

Add diced red onion, cucumber, bell pepper, parsley, lemon juice, olive oil, salt, and pepper to the bowl.

Mix well to combine.

Divide the chickpea salad evenly among the tortillas and wrap tightly.

Serve immediately or refrigerate until ready to eat.

Nutritional Info: Calories: 240 | Carbs: 35g | Protein: 8g | Fat: 8g | Potassium: 320mg | Sodium: 420mg | Cholesterol: 0mg

15. Vegetarian Chili

Servings: 6

Cooking Time: 45 minutes

Ingredients:

1 tablespoon olive oil

1 onion, diced

2 cloves garlic, minced

1 bell pepper, diced

1 zucchini, diced

1 cup diced tomatoes

1 can (15 oz) kidney beans, drained and rinsed

1 can (15 oz) black beans, drained and rinsed

2 cups vegetable broth

2 teaspoons chili powder

1 teaspoon cumin

Salt and pepper to taste

Preparation Method:

Heat olive oil in a large pot over medium heat.

Add diced onion, garlic, bell pepper, and zucchini. Cook until vegetables are softened.

Stir in diced tomatoes, kidney beans, black beans, vegetable broth, chili powder, cumin, salt, and pepper.

Bring to a boil, then reduce heat and simmer for 30 minutes, stirring occasionally.

Serve hot with your choice of toppings such as avocado, cilantro, or shredded cheese.

Nutritional Info: Calories: 280 | Carbs: 45g | Protein: 12g | Fat: 6g | Potassium: 650mg | Sodium: 490mg | Cholesterol: 0mg

16. Mediterranean Quinoa Salad

Servings: 4

Preparation Time: 20 minutes

Ingredients:

1 cup quinoa, cooked

1 cucumber, diced

1 cup cherry tomatoes, halved

1/2 cup Kalamata olives, sliced

1/4 cup red onion, thinly sliced

1/4 cup crumbled feta cheese

2 tablespoons chopped fresh parsley

2 tablespoons lemon juice

1 tablespoon olive oil

Salt and pepper to taste

Preparation Method:

In a large bowl, combine cooked quinoa, diced cucumber, cherry tomatoes, Kalamata olives, red onion, feta cheese, and parsley.

In a small bowl, whisk together lemon juice, olive oil, salt, and pepper to make the dressing.

Pour the dressing over the salad and toss to coat evenly.

Serve chilled or at room temperature.

Nutritional Info: Calories: 280 | Carbs: 35g | Protein: 8g | Fat: 12g | Potassium: 350mg | Sodium: 320mg | Cholesterol: 10mg

17. Eggplant and Tomato Pasta

Servings: 4

Cooking Time: 30 minutes

Ingredients:

8 oz whole wheat spaghetti

1 eggplant, diced

2 cups diced tomatoes

2 cloves garlic, minced

2 tablespoons olive oil

1/4 cup chopped fresh basil

Salt and pepper to taste

Preparation Method:

Cook spaghetti according to package instructions, then drain and set aside.

Heat olive oil in a large skillet over medium heat.

Add minced garlic and diced eggplant, cook until eggplant is softened.

Stir in diced tomatoes and cook for another 5-7 minutes until heated through.

Season with salt and pepper, then toss with cooked spaghetti.

Garnish with chopped fresh basil before serving.

Nutritional Info: Calories: 320 | Carbs: 45g | Protein: 10g | Fat: 12g | Potassium: 480mg | Sodium: 210mg | Cholesterol: 0mg

18. Spinach and Chickpea Curry

Servings: 4

Cooking Time: 25 minutes

Ingredients:

1 tablespoon olive oil and onion, diced

2 cloves garlic, minced and 1 tablespoon curry powder

1 teaspoon ground cumin and 1 can (15 oz) chickpeas, drained and rinsed

1 can (14 oz) diced tomatoes and 2 cups fresh spinach

Salt and pepper to taste

Preparation Method:

Heat olive oil in a large skillet over medium heat.

Add diced onion and minced garlic, cook until softened.

Stir in curry powder and ground cumin, cook for another minute until fragrant.

Add chickpeas and diced tomatoes to the skillet, bring to a simmer.

Stir in fresh spinach and cook until wilted.

Season with salt and pepper to taste.

Serve hot with rice or naan bread.

Nutritional Info: Calories: 250 | Carbs: 35g | Protein: 10g | Fat: 8g | Potassium: 420mg | Sodium: 480mg | Cholesterol: 0mg

19. Stuffed Bell Peppers

Servings: 4

Cooking Time: 45 minutes

Ingredients:

4 bell peppers, halved and seeds removed and 1 cup cooked quinoa

1 can (15 oz) black beans, drained and rinsed

1 cup diced tomatoes and 1/2 cup corn kernels

1/4 cup diced red onion and 1 teaspoon chili powder

1/2 teaspoon cumin and Salt and pepper to taste

1/2 cup shredded cheese (optional)

Preparation Method:

Preheat oven to 375°F (190°C) and grease a baking dish.

In a large bowl, mix cooked quinoa, black beans, diced tomatoes, corn kernels, diced red onion, chili powder, cumin, salt, and pepper.

Stuff each bell pepper half with the quinoa mixture and place in the baking dish.

Cover with foil and bake for 30 minutes.

Remove foil, sprinkle shredded cheese on top if desired, and bake for an additional 10-15 minutes until peppers are tender, cheese is melted and Serve hot.

Nutritional Info: Calories: 280 | Carbs: 45g | Protein: 12g | Fat: 6g | Potassium: 550mg | Sodium: 490mg | Cholesterol: 10mg

20. Vegetable and Lentil Curry

Servings: 4

Cooking Time: 35 minutes

Ingredients:

1 tablespoon olive oil and 1 onion, diced

2 cloves garlic, minced and 1 tablespoon curry powder

1 teaspoon ground cumin and 1 cup dried red lentils, rinsed

2 cups vegetable broth and 1 can (14 oz) diced tomatoes

2 cups mixed vegetables (such as carrots, bell peppers, and cauliflower)

Salt and pepper to taste

Preparation Method:

Heat olive oil in a large pot over medium heat.

Add diced onion and minced garlic, cook until softened.

Stir in curry powder and ground cumin, cook for another minute until fragrant.

Add dried red lentils, vegetable broth, diced tomatoes, and mixed vegetables to the pot.

Bring to a boil, then reduce heat and simmer for 20-25 minutes until lentils and vegetables are tender.

Season with salt and pepper to taste.

Serve hot with rice or naan bread.

Nutritional Info: Calories: 290 | Carbs: 45g | Protein: 14g | Fat: 6g | Potassium: 640mg | Sodium: 480mg | Cholesterol: 0mg

42 VEGETARIAN DIABETIC RENAL DIET COOKBOOK

CHAPTER FIVE: Dinner Recipes

21. Grilled Portobello Mushroom Steaks

Servings: 2

Cooking Time: 20 minutes

Ingredients:

2 large portobello mushrooms

2 tablespoons balsamic vinegar

2 tablespoons olive oil

2 cloves garlic, minced

1 teaspoon dried thyme

Salt and pepper to taste

Preparation Method:

Clean the portobello mushrooms and remove the stems.

In a small bowl, whisk together balsamic vinegar, olive oil, minced garlic, dried thyme, salt, and pepper to make the marinade.

Brush the marinade over both sides of the mushrooms and let them marinate for 10 minutes.

Preheat grill to medium heat and grill the mushrooms for 5-7 minutes on each side until tender.

Serve hot.

Nutritional Info: Calories: 150 | Carbs: 10g | Protein: 5g | Fat: 10g | Potassium: 600mg | Sodium: 15mg | Cholesterol: 0mg

22. Vegetable Stir-Fry with Tofu

Servings: 4

Cooking Time: 20 minutes

Ingredients:

1 block (14 oz) extra-firm tofu, pressed and cubed

2 tablespoons low-sodium soy sauce

1 tablespoon sesame oil

1 tablespoon olive oil

2 cloves garlic, minced

1 teaspoon grated ginger

2 cups mixed vegetables (such as bell peppers, broccoli, carrots)

Cooked brown rice for serving

Preparation Method:

In a bowl, toss cubed tofu with low-sodium soy sauce and sesame oil.

Heat olive oil in a large skillet or wok over medium-high heat.

Add minced garlic and grated ginger, cook for 1 minute until fragrant.

Add tofu to the skillet and cook until browned on all sides.

Stir in mixed vegetables and cook until tender-crisp.

Serve hot over cooked brown rice.

Nutritional Info: Calories: 250 | Carbs: 20g | Protein: 15g | Fat: 12g | Potassium: 400mg | Sodium: 300mg | Cholesterol: 0mg

23. Spaghetti Squash with Marinara Sauce

Servings: 4

Cooking Time: 45 minutes

Ingredients:

1 large spaghetti squash

2 cups marinara sauce (store-bought or homemade)

1 tablespoon olive oil

Salt and pepper to taste

Fresh basil for garnish

Preparation Method:

Preheat oven to 400°F (200°C).

Cut spaghetti squash in half lengthwise and scoop out the seeds.

Drizzle olive oil over the cut sides of the squash and season with salt and pepper.

Place squash halves cut-side down on a baking sheet and roast for 30-40 minutes until tender.

Scrape the flesh of the squash with a fork to create "spaghetti" strands.

Heat marinara sauce in a saucepan over medium heat until warmed through.

Serve spaghetti squash topped with marinara sauce and garnished with fresh basil.

Nutritional Info: Calories: 180 | Carbs: 30g | Protein: 4g | Fat: 6g | Potassium: 380mg | Sodium: 400mg | Cholesterol: 0mg

24. Black Bean and Sweet Potato Tacos

Servings: 4

Cooking Time: 30 minutes

Ingredients:

1 tablespoon olive oil

1 onion, diced

2 cloves garlic, minced

2 cups diced sweet potatoes

1 can (15 oz) black beans, drained and rinsed

1 teaspoon chili powder

1/2 teaspoon cumin

1/4 teaspoon paprika

Salt and pepper to taste

8 small corn tortillas

Toppings: diced tomatoes, avocado, cilantro

Preparation Method:

Heat olive oil in a large skillet over medium heat.

Add diced onion and minced garlic, cook until softened.

Stir in diced sweet potatoes and cook until tender, about 10 minutes.

Add black beans, chili powder, cumin, paprika, salt, and pepper to the skillet. Cook for another 5 minutes until heated through.

Warm corn tortillas in a separate skillet or microwave.

Spoon sweet potato and black bean mixture onto each tortilla.

Top with diced tomatoes, avocado, and cilantro.

Nutritional Info: Calories: 280 | Carbs: 45g | Protein: 8g | Fat: 7g | Potassium: 550mg | Sodium: 240mg | Cholesterol: 0mg

25. Mushroom and Spinach Risotto

Servings: 4

Cooking Time: 45 minutes

Ingredients:

1 tablespoon olive oil

1 onion, diced

2 cloves garlic, minced

1 cup Arborio rice

4 cups vegetable broth, heated

8 oz mushrooms, sliced

2 cups fresh spinach

1/4 cup grated Parmesan cheese

Salt and pepper to taste

Preparation Method:

Heat olive oil in a large skillet or Dutch oven over medium heat.

Add diced onion and minced garlic, cook until softened.

Stir in Arborio rice and cook for 1-2 minutes until lightly toasted.

Gradually add heated vegetable broth to the skillet, 1 cup at a time, stirring frequently until absorbed.

Add sliced mushrooms and continue adding broth and stirring until rice is creamy and tender, about 25-30 minutes.

Stir in fresh spinach until wilted, then remove from heat.

Stir in grated Parmesan cheese, season with salt and pepper to taste.

Nutritional Info: Calories: 300 | Carbs: 50g | Protein: 8g | Fat: 7g | Potassium: 400mg | Sodium: 680mg | Cholesterol: 5mg

26. Stuffed Bell Peppers with Quinoa and Black Beans

Servings: 4

Cooking Time: 45 minutes

Ingredients:

4 bell peppers, halved and seeds removed

1 cup cooked quinoa

1 can (15 oz) black beans, drained and rinsed

1 cup diced tomatoes

1/2 cup corn kernels

1/4 cup diced red onion

1 teaspoon chili powder

1/2 teaspoon cumin

Salt and pepper to taste

1/2 cup shredded cheese (optional)

Preparation Method:

Preheat oven to 375°F (190°C) and grease a baking dish.

In a large bowl, mix cooked quinoa, black beans, diced tomatoes, corn kernels, diced red onion, chili powder, cumin, salt, and pepper.

Stuff each bell pepper half with the quinoa mixture and place in the baking dish.

Cover with foil and bake for 30 minutes.

Remove foil, sprinkle shredded cheese on top if desired, and bake for an additional 10-15 minutes until peppers are tender and cheese is melted.

Serve hot.

Nutritional Info: Calories: 280 | Carbs: 45g | Protein: 12g | Fat: 6g | Potassium: 550mg | Sodium: 490mg | Cholesterol: 10mg

27. Vegetarian Lentil Shepherd's Pie

Servings: 6

Cooking Time: 50 minutes

Ingredients:

2 cups cooked lentils

2 cups mixed vegetables (such as carrots, peas, corn)

1 onion, diced

2 cloves garlic, minced

2 tablespoons tomato paste

1 tablespoon Worcestershire sauce (optional)

2 cups mashed potatoes

Salt and pepper to taste

Preparation Method:

Preheat oven to 375°F (190°C).

In a skillet, sauté diced onion and minced garlic until softened.

Add cooked lentils, mixed vegetables, tomato paste, and Worcestershire sauce to the skillet. Cook until heated through.

Season with salt and pepper to taste.

Transfer the lentil and vegetable mixture to a baking dish.

Spread mashed potatoes over the top of the mixture.

Bake for 25-30 minutes until the mashed potatoes are golden brown.

Nutritional Info: Calories: 280 | Carbs: 50g | Protein: 12g | Fat: 4g | Potassium: 600mg | Sodium: 310mg | Cholesterol: 0mg

28. Eggplant Parmesan

Servings: 4

Cooking Time: 50 minutes

Ingredients:

1 large eggplant, sliced into rounds

1 cup whole wheat breadcrumbs

1/4 cup grated Parmesan cheese

2 eggs, beaten

2 cups marinara sauce (store-bought or homemade)

1 cup shredded mozzarella cheese

Salt and pepper to taste

Preparation Method:

Preheat oven to 375°F (190°C) and grease a baking dish.

Season eggplant slices with salt and let sit for 10 minutes to release excess moisture. Pat dry with paper towels.

In one bowl, combine whole wheat breadcrumbs and grated Parmesan cheese. In another bowl, place beaten eggs.

Dip eggplant slices in beaten eggs, then coat with breadcrumb mixture.

Place coated eggplant slices on the prepared baking dish and bake for 20-25 minutes until golden brown and crispy.

Remove from oven and top each slice with marinara sauce and shredded mozzarella cheese.

Return to oven and bake for another 15-20 minutes until cheese is melted and bubbly.

Nutritional Info: Calories: 320 | Carbs: 35g | Protein: 15g | Fat: 14g | Potassium: 580mg | Sodium: 620mg | Cholesterol: 100mg

29. Vegetarian Chili

Servings: 6

Cooking Time: 45 minutes

Ingredients:

1 tablespoon olive oil

1 onion, diced

2 cloves garlic, minced

1 bell pepper, diced

1 zucchini, diced

1 cup diced tomatoes

1 can (15 oz) kidney beans, drained and rinsed

1 can (15 oz) black beans, drained and rinsed

2 cups vegetable broth

2 teaspoons chili powder

1 teaspoon cumin

Salt and pepper to taste

Preparation Method:

Heat olive oil in a large pot over medium heat.

Add diced onion, garlic, bell pepper, and zucchini. Cook until vegetables are softened.

Stir in diced tomatoes, kidney beans, black beans, vegetable broth, chili powder, cumin, salt, and pepper.

Bring to a boil, then reduce heat and simmer for 30 minutes, stirring occasionally.

Serve hot with your choice of toppings such as avocado, cilantro, or shredded cheese.

Nutritional Info: Calories: 280 | Carbs: 45g | Protein: 12g | Fat: 6g | Potassium: 650mg | Sodium: 490mg | Cholesterol: 0mg

30. Mediterranean Stuffed Peppers

Servings: 4

Cooking Time: 50 minutes

Ingredients:

4 bell peppers, halved and seeds removed

1 cup cooked quinoa

1 can (15 oz) chickpeas, drained and rinsed

1/2 cup diced tomatoes

1/4 cup chopped fresh parsley

1/4 cup crumbled feta cheese

2 tablespoons olive oil

1 tablespoon lemon juice

Salt and pepper to taste

Preparation Method:

Preheat oven to 375°F (190°C) and grease a baking dish.

In a large bowl, mix cooked quinoa, chickpeas, diced tomatoes, chopped fresh parsley, crumbled feta cheese, olive oil, lemon juice, salt, and pepper.

Stuff each bell pepper half with the quinoa mixture and place in the baking dish.

Cover with foil and bake for 30 minutes.

Remove foil and bake for an additional 15-20 minutes until peppers are tender.

Serve hot.

Nutritional Info: Calories: 320 | Carbs: 45g | Protein: 12g | Fat: 10g | Potassium: 550mg | Sodium: 320mg | Cholesterol: 15mg

CHAPTER SIX: Snacks and Appetizers

31. Hummus with Vegetable Sticks

Servings: 4

Preparation Time: 10 minutes

Ingredients:

1 can (15 oz) chickpeas, drained and rinsed

2 cloves garlic, minced

2 tablespoons tahini

2 tablespoons lemon juice

1 tablespoon olive oil

Salt and pepper to taste

Assorted vegetable sticks (carrots, celery, bell peppers)

Preparation Method:

In a food processor, combine chickpeas, minced garlic, tahini, lemon juice, olive oil, salt, and pepper.

Blend until smooth, adding water if needed to reach desired consistency.

Serve hummus with assorted vegetable sticks for dipping.

Nutritional Info: Calories: 120 | Carbs: 15g | Protein: 5g | Fat: 5g | Potassium: 200mg | Sodium: 120mg | Cholesterol: 0mg

32. Guacamole with Whole Wheat Pita Chips

Servings: 4

Preparation Time: 15 minutes

Ingredients:

2 ripe avocados, peeled and mashed

1 tomato, diced

1/4 cup diced red onion

1/4 cup chopped fresh cilantro

1 tablespoon lime juice

Salt and pepper to taste

4 whole wheat pita bread, cut into wedges

Preparation Method:

In a bowl, combine mashed avocados, diced tomato, diced red onion, chopped cilantro, lime juice, salt, and pepper.

Mix until well combined.

Serve guacamole with whole wheat pita chips for dipping.

Nutritional Info: Calories: 180 | Carbs: 20g | Protein: 4g | Fat: 10g | Potassium: 350mg | Sodium: 150mg | Cholesterol: 0mg

33. Cucumber and Tomato Salad

Servings: 2

Preparation Time: 10 minutes

Ingredients:

1 cucumber, diced

1 tomato, diced

2 tablespoons chopped fresh parsley

1 tablespoon olive oil

1 tablespoon lemon juice

Salt and pepper to taste

Preparation Method:

In a bowl, combine diced cucumber, diced tomato, chopped parsley, olive oil, lemon juice, salt, and pepper.

Toss until well combined.

Serve chilled.

Nutritional Info: Calories: 80 | Carbs: 8g | Protein: 2g | Fat: 5g | Potassium: 250mg | Sodium: 10mg | Cholesterol: 0mg

34. Greek Yogurt Dip with Sliced Bell Peppers

Servings: 4

Preparation Time: 5 minutes

Ingredients:

1 cup Greek yogurt

1 tablespoon chopped fresh dill

1 tablespoon lemon juice

Salt and pepper to taste

Assorted sliced bell peppers (red, yellow, green)

Preparation Method:

In a bowl, combine Greek yogurt, chopped dill, lemon juice, salt, and pepper.

Mix until well combined.

Serve dip with assorted sliced bell peppers for dipping.

Nutritional Info: Calories: 60 | Carbs: 5g | Protein: 8g | Fat: 2g | Potassium: 150mg | Sodium: 40mg | Cholesterol: 5mg

35. Roasted Chickpeas

Servings: 4

Preparation Time: 40 minutes

Ingredients:

1 can (15 oz) chickpeas, drained and rinsed

1 tablespoon olive oil

1 teaspoon paprika

1/2 teaspoon garlic powder

1/2 teaspoon cumin

Salt and pepper to taste

Preparation Method:

Preheat oven to 400°F (200°C).

Pat chickpeas dry with paper towels and remove any loose skins.

In a bowl, toss chickpeas with olive oil, paprika, garlic powder, cumin, salt, and pepper.

Spread chickpeas in a single layer on a baking sheet.

Roast in the oven for 30-35 minutes, stirring occasionally, until crispy.

Let cool before serving.

Nutritional Info: Calories: 120 | Carbs: 15g | Protein: 5g | Fat: 5g | Potassium: 200mg | Sodium: 150mg | Cholesterol: 0mg

36. Stuffed Cherry Tomatoes

Servings: 4

Preparation Time: 15 minutes

Ingredients:

16 cherry tomatoes

1/2 cup crumbled feta cheese

2 tablespoons chopped fresh basil

1 tablespoon olive oil

Salt and pepper to taste

Preparation Method:

Cut the top off each cherry tomato and scoop out the seeds to create a hollow cavity.

In a bowl, combine crumbled feta cheese, chopped basil, olive oil, salt, and pepper.

Stuff each cherry tomato with the feta mixture.

Serve chilled.

Nutritional Info: Calories: 60 | Carbs: 3g | Protein: 2g | Fat: 4g | Potassium: 150mg | Sodium: 100mg | Cholesterol: 10mg

37. Spinach and Feta Phyllo Triangles

Servings: 6

Preparation Time: 30 minutes

Ingredients:

6 sheets phyllo dough, thawed

2 cups fresh spinach, chopped

1/2 cup crumbled feta cheese

2 tablespoons chopped fresh dill

1 tablespoon olive oil

Salt and pepper to taste

Preparation Method:

Preheat oven to 375°F (190°C) and line a baking sheet with parchment paper.

In a bowl, combine chopped spinach, crumbled feta cheese, chopped dill, olive oil, salt, and pepper.

Place one sheet of phyllo dough on a clean surface and brush lightly with olive oil.

Place another sheet of phyllo dough on top and brush with olive oil.

Cut the stacked phyllo sheets into 4 equal squares.

Place a spoonful of the spinach mixture in the center of each square.

Fold each square into a triangle and place on the prepared baking sheet.

Bake for 15-20 minutes until golden brown and crispy.

Nutritional Info: Calories: 150 | Carbs: 15g | Protein: 4g | Fat: 8g | Potassium: 200mg | Sodium: 200mg | Cholesterol: 15mg

38. Cucumber Roll-Ups

Servings: 4

Preparation Time: 15 minutes

Ingredients:

1 large cucumber

1/2 cup hummus

1/4 cup shredded carrots

1/4 cup sliced red bell pepper

1/4 cup sliced cucumber

Preparation Method:

Slice the cucumber lengthwise into thin strips using a vegetable peeler or mandoline slicer.

Spread a thin layer of hummus onto each cucumber strip.

Place shredded carrots, sliced red bell pepper, and sliced cucumber on one end of each cucumber strip.

Roll up the cucumber strips tightly to form roll-ups.

Secure with toothpicks if necessary.

Serve chilled.

Nutritional Info: Calories: 60 | Carbs: 8g | Protein: 2g | Fat: 3g | Potassium: 150mg | Sodium: 100mg | Cholesterol: 0mg

39. Stuffed Mushrooms

Servings: 4

Preparation Time: 25 minutes

Ingredients:

12 large mushrooms, stems removed and chopped

1/2 cup breadcrumbs

1/4 cup grated Parmesan cheese

2 cloves garlic, minced

2 tablespoons chopped fresh parsley

1 tablespoon olive oil

Salt and pepper to taste

Preparation Method:

Preheat oven to 375°F (190°C) and line a baking sheet with parchment paper.

In a bowl, combine chopped mushroom stems, breadcrumbs, grated Parmesan cheese, minced garlic, chopped parsley, olive oil, salt, and pepper.

Mix until well combined.

Stuff each mushroom cap with the breadcrumb mixture.

Place stuffed mushrooms on the prepared baking sheet.

Bake for 15-20 minutes until mushrooms are tender and tops are golden brown.

Nutritional Info: Calories: 80 | Carbs: 10g | Protein: 4g | Fat: 3g | Potassium: 200mg | Sodium: 150mg | Cholesterol: 5mg

40. Edamame Salad

Servings: 4

Preparation Time: 10 minutes

Ingredients:

2 cups cooked edamame beans

1 cup diced cucumber

1/4 cup diced red onion

2 tablespoons chopped fresh cilantro

1 tablespoon sesame oil

1 tablespoon rice vinegar

Salt and pepper to taste

Preparation Method:

In a bowl, combine cooked edamame beans, diced cucumber, diced red onion, chopped cilantro, sesame oil, rice vinegar, salt, and pepper.

Toss until well combined.

Serve chilled.

Nutritional Info: Calories: 150 | Carbs: 10g | Protein: 10g | Fat: 8g | Potassium: 300mg | Sodium: 10mg | Cholesterol: 0mg

CHAPTER SEVEN: Desserts

41. Banana Oatmeal Cookies

Servings: 12 cookies

Preparation Time: 25 minutes

Ingredients:

2 ripe bananas, mashed

1 cup rolled oats and 1/4 cup chopped walnuts

1/4 cup raisins and 1 teaspoon cinnamon

Preparation Method:

Preheat oven to 350°F (175°C) and line a baking sheet with parchment paper.

In a bowl, combine mashed bananas, rolled oats, chopped walnuts, raisins, and cinnamon. Mix well.

Drop spoonfuls of the mixture onto the prepared baking sheet and flatten slightly with the back of a spoon.

Bake for 15-18 minutes until golden brown.

Let cool before serving.

Nutritional Info: Calories: 80 | Carbs: 15g | Protein: 2g | Fat: 2g | Potassium: 120mg | Sodium: 0mg | Cholesterol: 0mg

42. Greek Yogurt Parfait with Berries

Servings: 2

Preparation Time: 10 minutes

Ingredients:

1 cup Greek yogurt

1/2 cup mixed berries (strawberries, blueberries, raspberries)

2 tablespoons chopped nuts (almonds, walnuts)

1 tablespoon honey (optional)

Preparation Method:

In two glasses or bowls, layer Greek yogurt, mixed berries, and chopped nuts.

Drizzle honey over the top if desired.

Serve immediately.

Nutritional Info: Calories: 150 | Carbs: 15g | Protein: 10g | Fat: 6g | Potassium: 200mg | Sodium: 40mg | Cholesterol: 5mg

43. Baked Apples with Cinnamon

Servings: 4

Preparation Time: 30 minutes

Ingredients:

4 apples

1/4 cup chopped nuts (pecans, almonds)

2 tablespoons raisins

1 tablespoon honey

1 teaspoon cinnamon

Preparation Method:

Preheat oven to 375°F (190°C).

Core the apples and place them in a baking dish.

In a bowl, combine chopped nuts, raisins, honey, and cinnamon.

Stuff each apple with the nut mixture.

Bake for 20-25 minutes until apples are tender.

Serve warm.

Nutritional Info: Calories: 120 | Carbs: 25g | Protein: 2g | Fat: 3g | Potassium: 200mg | Sodium: 0mg | Cholesterol: 0mg

44. Chia Seed Pudding

Servings: 4

Preparation Time: 5 minutes (+ chilling time)

Ingredients:

1/4 cup chia seeds

1 cup almond milk (unsweetened)

1 tablespoon honey (optional)

1/2 teaspoon vanilla extract

Fresh fruit for topping (berries, sliced banana)

Preparation Method:

In a bowl, whisk together chia seeds, almond milk, honey (if using), and vanilla extract.

Let sit for 5 minutes, then whisk again to prevent clumping.

Cover and refrigerate for at least 2 hours or overnight until thickened.

Serve chilled with fresh fruit toppings.

Nutritional Info: Calories: 80 | Carbs: 8g | Protein: 3g | Fat: 4g | Potassium: 100mg | Sodium: 50mg | Cholesterol: 0mg

45. Frozen Banana Bites

Servings: 4

Preparation Time: 1 hour

Ingredients:

2 ripe bananas

1/4 cup dark chocolate chips

1/4 cup chopped nuts (walnuts, almonds)

Preparation Method:

Peel the bananas and cut them into bite-sized pieces.

Insert a toothpick into each banana piece and place them on a baking sheet lined with parchment paper.

Melt dark chocolate chips in a microwave-safe bowl in 30-second intervals, stirring in between until smooth.

Dip each banana piece into the melted chocolate, then sprinkle with chopped nuts.

Place the baking sheet in the freezer for at least 1 hour until the chocolate is set.

Serve frozen.

Nutritional Info: Calories: 100 | Carbs: 15g | Protein: 2g | Fat: 4g | Potassium: 200mg | Sodium: 0mg | Cholesterol: 0mg

46. Coconut Rice Pudding

Servings: 4

Preparation Time: 40 minutes

Ingredients:

1/2 cup Arborio rice

2 cups coconut milk (unsweetened)

1/4 cup honey

1 teaspoon vanilla extract

1/4 cup shredded coconut (unsweetened)

Preparation Method:

In a saucepan, combine Arborio rice and coconut milk.

Bring to a simmer over medium heat, then reduce heat to low and cook for 30-35 minutes, stirring occasionally, until rice is tender and creamy.

Stir in honey, vanilla extract, and shredded coconut.

Cook for another 5 minutes until thickened.

Serve warm or chilled.

Nutritional Info: Calories: 200 | Carbs: 30g | Protein: 2g | Fat: 8g | Potassium: 100mg | Sodium: 10mg | Cholesterol: 0mg

47. Berry Sorbet

Servings: 4

Preparation Time: 10 minutes (+ freezing time)

Ingredients:

2 cups mixed berries (strawberries, blueberries, raspberries)

1/4 cup honey

1 tablespoon lemon juice

Preparation Method:

In a blender, combine mixed berries, honey, and lemon juice.

Blend until smooth.

Pour the mixture into a shallow dish and freeze for 2-3 hours, stirring every 30 minutes, until firm but scoopable.

Serve scoops of sorbet in bowls.

Nutritional Info: Calories: 70 | Carbs: 20g | Protein: 1g | Fat: 0g | Potassium: 150mg | Sodium: 0mg | Cholesterol: 0mg

48. Chocolate Avocado Mousse

Servings: 4

Preparation Time: 15 minutes

Ingredients:

2 ripe avocados

1/4 cup cocoa powder

1/4 cup honey

1 teaspoon vanilla extract

Pinch of salt

Preparation Method:

Scoop the flesh of the avocados into a food processor.

Add cocoa powder, honey, vanilla extract, and a pinch of salt.

Blend until smooth and creamy.

Divide the mousse into serving bowls.

Chill in the refrigerator for at least 1 hour before serving.

Nutritional Info: Calories: 160 | Carbs: 20g | Protein: 2g | Fat: 10g | Potassium: 300mg | Sodium: 5mg | Cholesterol: 0mg

49. Fruit Salad with Mint-Lime Dressing

Servings: 4

Preparation Time: 15 minutes

Ingredients:

2 cups mixed fruit (melon, pineapple, grapes, berries)

2 tablespoons freshly squeezed lime juice

1 tablespoon honey

1 tablespoon chopped fresh mint

Preparation Method:

In a bowl, combine mixed fruit.

In a small bowl, whisk together lime juice, honey, and chopped mint.

Pour the dressing over the fruit and toss gently to coat.

Serve chilled.

Nutritional Info: Calories: 80 | Carbs: 20g | Protein: 1g | Fat: 0g | Potassium: 150mg | Sodium: 0mg | Cholesterol: 0mg

50. Baked Pears with Cinnamon

Servings: 4

Preparation Time: 30 minutes

Ingredients:

4 ripe pears

1/4 cup chopped nuts (walnuts, almonds)

2 tablespoons honey

1 teaspoon cinnamon

Preparation Method:

Preheat oven to 375°F (190°C) and line a baking dish with parchment paper.

Slice the pears in half lengthwise and remove the cores.

Place the pear halves in the baking dish, cut side up.

In a small bowl, combine chopped nuts, honey, and cinnamon.

Spoon the nut mixture into the center of each pear half.

Bake for 20-25 minutes until pears are tender.

Serve warm.

Nutritional Info: Calories: 120 | Carbs: 25g | Protein: 2g | Fat: 3g | Potassium: 200mg | Sodium: 0mg | Cholesterol: 0mg

CHAPTER EIGHT: Beverages

51. Cucumber Mint Cooler

Servings: 2

Preparation Time: 10 minutes

Ingredients:

1 cucumber, peeled and chopped

1/4 cup fresh mint leaves

2 cups water

1 tablespoon lemon juice

Ice cubes

Preparation Method:

In a blender, combine chopped cucumber, fresh mint leaves, water, and lemon juice.

Blend until smooth.

Strain the mixture to remove any pulp.

Serve over ice cubes.

Nutritional Info: Calories: 10 | Carbs: 2g | Protein: 0g | Fat: 0g | Potassium: 100mg | Sodium: 0mg | Cholesterol: 0mg

52. Berry Blast Smoothie

Servings: 2

Preparation Time: 5 minutes

Ingredients:

1 cup mixed berries (strawberries, blueberries, raspberries)

1 ripe banana

1 cup unsweetened almond milk

1/4 cup Greek yogurt

1 tablespoon honey (optional)

Ice cubes

Preparation Method:

In a blender, combine mixed berries, banana, almond milk, Greek yogurt, and honey (if using).

Blend until smooth.

Add ice cubes and blend again until desired consistency is reached.

Serve immediately.

Nutritional Info: Calories: 100 | Carbs: 20g | Protein: 3g | Fat: 2g | Potassium: 200mg | Sodium: 80mg | Cholesterol: 0mg

53. Watermelon Lime Refresher

Servings: 2

Preparation Time: 10 minutes

Ingredients:

2 cups diced watermelon

Juice of 2 limes

2 cups water

1 tablespoon honey (optional)

Mint leaves for garnish

Ice cubes

Preparation Method:

In a blender, combine diced watermelon, lime juice, water, and honey (if using).

Blend until smooth.

Strain the mixture to remove any pulp.

Serve over ice cubes, garnished with mint leaves.

Nutritional Info: Calories: 50 | Carbs: 15g | Protein: 1g | Fat: 0g | Potassium: 150mg | Sodium: 0mg | Cholesterol: 0mg

54. Green Tea Lemonade

Servings: 2

Preparation Time: 15 minutes

Ingredients:

2 green tea bags

2 cups hot water

Juice of 1 lemon

1 tablespoon honey (optional)

Ice cubes

Preparation Method:

Steep green tea bags in hot water for 5-7 minutes.

Remove tea bags and let the tea cool to room temperature.

Stir in lemon juice and honey (if using).

Chill in the refrigerator until cold.

Serve over ice cubes.

Nutritional Info: Calories: 10 | Carbs: 3g | Protein: 0g | Fat: 0g | Potassium: 50mg | Sodium: 0mg | Cholesterol: 0mg

55. Pineapple Ginger Punch

Servings: 2

Preparation Time: 10 minutes

Ingredients:

1 cup diced pineapple

1-inch piece of ginger, peeled and chopped

2 cups water

Juice of 1 lime

1 tablespoon honey (optional)

Ice cubes

Preparation Method:

In a blender, combine diced pineapple, chopped ginger, water, lime juice, and honey (if using).

Blend until smooth.

Strain the mixture to remove any pulp.

Serve over ice cubes.

Nutritional Info: Calories: 60 | Carbs: 15g | Protein: 1g | Fat: 0g | Potassium: 150mg | Sodium: 0mg | Cholesterol: 0mg

56. Coconut Watermelon Cooler

Servings: 2

Preparation Time: 10 minutes

Ingredients:

2 cups diced watermelon

1/2 cup coconut water

Juice of 1 lime

1 tablespoon honey (optional)

Ice cubes

Preparation Method:

In a blender, combine diced watermelon, coconut water, lime juice, and honey (if using).

Blend until smooth.

Strain the mixture to remove any pulp.

Serve over ice cubes.

Nutritional Info: Calories: 50 | Carbs: 15g | Protein: 1g | Fat: 0g | Potassium: 150mg | Sodium: 50mg | Cholesterol: 0mg

57. Cranberry Orange Spritzer

Servings: 2

Preparation Time: 5 minutes

Ingredients:

1 cup cranberry juice (unsweetened)

1/2 cup sparkling water

Juice of 1 orange

Orange slices for garnish

Ice cubes

Preparation Method:

In a pitcher, combine cranberry juice, sparkling water, and orange juice.

Stir to mix well.

Serve over ice cubes, garnished with orange slices.

Nutritional Info: Calories: 60 | Carbs: 15g | Protein: 0g | Fat: 0g | Potassium: 100mg | Sodium: 10mg | Cholesterol: 0mg

58. Minty Lime Iced Tea

Servings: 2

Preparation Time: 15 minutes

Ingredients:

2 green tea bags

2 cups hot water

Juice of 2 limes

2 tablespoons chopped fresh mint

1 tablespoon honey (optional)

Ice cubes

Preparation Method:

Steep green tea bags in hot water for 5-7 minutes.

Remove tea bags and let the tea cool to room temperature.

Stir in lime juice, chopped mint, and honey (if using).

Chill in the refrigerator until cold.

Serve over ice cubes.

Nutritional Info: Calories: 10 | Carbs: 3g | Protein: 0g | Fat: 0g | Potassium: 50mg | Sodium: 0mg | Cholesterol: 0mg

59. Peach Basil Sparkler

Servings: 2

Preparation Time: 10 minutes

Ingredients:

1 ripe peach, pitted and sliced

1/4 cup fresh basil leaves

1 cup sparkling water

Juice of 1 lemon

1 tablespoon honey (optional)

Ice cubes

Preparation Method:

In a blender, combine sliced peach, basil leaves, sparkling water, lemon juice, and honey (if using).

Blend until smooth.

Strain the mixture to remove any pulp.

Serve over ice cubes.

Nutritional Info: Calories: 50 | Carbs: 15g | Protein: 1g | Fat: 0g | Potassium: 150mg | Sodium: 0mg | Cholesterol: 0mg

60. Tropical Green Smoothie

Servings: 2

Preparation Time: 5 minutes

Ingredients:

1 cup spinach leaves

1/2 cup diced pineapple

1/2 ripe banana

1/2 cup unsweetened coconut milk

1/2 cup water

Ice cubes

Preparation Method:

In a blender, combine spinach leaves, diced pineapple, banana, coconut milk, and water.

Blend until smooth.

Add ice cubes and blend again until desired consistency is reached.

Serve immediately.

Nutritional Info: Calories: 70 | Carbs: 15g | Protein: 1g | Fat: 1g | Potassium: 200mg | Sodium: 50mg | Cholesterol: 0mg

CONCLUSION

In closing, the journey towards better health and well-being through the Vegetarian Diabetic Renal Diet Cookbook has been one of discovery, empowerment, and transformation. As we turn the final pages of this culinary companion, we're reminded of the incredible power of food to heal, nourish, and rejuvenate both body and soul.

Through the vibrant array of recipes meticulously crafted to cater to the unique dietary needs of those managing diabetes and renal health, this cookbook has transcended the realm of mere culinary guide and emerged as a beacon of hope and possibility. It has shown us that flavorful, satisfying meals need not be sacrificed in the pursuit of health, but rather, can be seamlessly integrated into a lifestyle of wellness and vitality.

With each page turned, we've embarked on a culinary odyssey that celebrates the bounty of nature's offerings – from the crisp crunch of fresh vegetables to the hearty warmth of whole grains and legumes. We've embraced the rich tapestry of flavors and textures that plant-based ingredients have to offer, reveling in the endless possibilities for creativity and indulgence they afford us.

But beyond the delectable dishes and tantalizing aromas lies a deeper message – one of empowerment and self-care. By embracing the principles of mindful eating, portion control, and balanced nutrition, we've taken control of our health destiny, charting a course towards a future filled with vitality and vigor.

As we bid farewell to the Vegetarian Diabetic Renal Diet Cookbook, let us carry forward the lessons learned and the flavors savored. Let us continue to explore, experiment, and innovate in the kitchen, knowing that each meal we prepare is a testament to our commitment to health and happiness.

May this cookbook serve as a constant companion on your journey to wellness, offering guidance, inspiration, and, above all, a delicious reminder that good food is the foundation upon which a vibrant life is built. Here's to your health, your happiness, and the culinary adventures that lie ahead. Bon appétit!

BONUS: 30 DAY MEAL PLAN

Day 1:

Breakfast: Scrambled tofu with spinach and mushrooms, whole grain toast

Lunch: Lentil soup with a side of mixed green salad

Dinner: Baked eggplant Parmesan with quinoa and steamed broccoli

Day 2:

Breakfast: Greek yogurt with berries and a sprinkle of chopped nuts

Lunch: Chickpea salad with cucumber, cherry tomatoes, and feta cheese

Dinner: Stuffed bell peppers with brown rice and black beans

Day 3:

Breakfast: Oatmeal topped with sliced banana and almonds

Lunch: Vegetable stir-fry with tofu over brown rice

Dinner: Spinach and ricotta stuffed shells with a side of roasted Brussels sprouts

Day 4:

Breakfast: Smoothie made with spinach, kale, banana, and almond milk

Lunch: Quinoa salad with roasted vegetables and a lemon tahini dressing

Dinner: Vegetable curry with cauliflower rice

Day 5:

Breakfast: Avocado toast on whole grain bread with cherry tomatoes

Lunch: Caprese salad with fresh mozzarella, tomatoes, and basil

Dinner: Lentil and vegetable stew with a side of steamed asparagus

Day 6:

Breakfast: Chia seed pudding topped with sliced strawberries

Lunch: Black bean and corn salad with avocado and lime dressing

Dinner: Ratatouille served with a side of quinoa pilaf

Day 7:

Breakfast: Whole grain pancakes with blueberry compote

Lunch: Spinach and feta stuffed mushrooms with a side of roasted sweet potatoes

Dinner: Cauliflower steak with chimichurri sauce and roasted carrots

Day 8:

Breakfast: Breakfast burrito with scrambled tofu, black beans, and salsa

Lunch: Mediterranean quinoa bowl with olives, artichokes, and hummus

Dinner: Zucchini noodles with marinara sauce and vegan meatballs

Day 9:

Breakfast: Overnight oats with sliced peaches and a drizzle of honey

Lunch: Spinach and white bean salad with roasted red peppers and balsamic vinaigrette

Dinner: Portobello mushroom burgers with sweet potato fries

Day 10:

Breakfast: Berry smoothie bowl topped with granola and coconut flakes

Lunch: Greek salad with tofu feta, cucumbers, and Kalamata olives

Dinner: Vegetable paella with a side of steamed green beans

Day 11:

Breakfast: Whole wheat toast with almond butter and sliced apples

Lunch: Roasted vegetable wrap with hummus and arugula

Dinner: Stuffed acorn squash with quinoa, cranberries, and walnuts

Day 12:

Breakfast: Tofu scramble breakfast burrito with salsa and avocado

Lunch: Asian-inspired tofu and vegetable stir-fry with brown rice

Dinner: Spaghetti squash with marinara sauce and a side of garlic bread

Day 13:

Breakfast: Smoothie made with spinach, banana, pineapple, and coconut milk

Lunch: Spinach and strawberry salad with almonds and a balsamic glaze

Dinner: Veggie burger on a whole grain bun with roasted cauliflower

Day 14:

Breakfast: Whole grain waffles with mixed berries and maple syrup

Lunch: Quinoa tabbouleh with cucumber, tomatoes, and parsley

Dinner: Stuffed portobello mushrooms with a side of roasted root vegetables

Day 15:

Breakfast: Avocado and tomato toast on whole grain bread

Lunch: Lentil salad with roasted vegetables and a lemon tahini dressing

Dinner: Vegetable lasagna with a side of steamed broccoli

Day 16:

Breakfast: Overnight chia seed pudding with mango and shredded coconut

Lunch: Greek-style stuffed peppers with couscous and feta cheese

Dinner: Butternut squash risotto with a side of sautéed spinach

Day 17:

Breakfast: Whole grain oatmeal with sliced strawberries and almonds

Lunch: Spinach and chickpea salad with roasted red peppers and feta cheese

Dinner: Stir-fried tofu and mixed vegetables with brown rice

Day 18:

Breakfast: Smoothie bowl topped with sliced banana, granola, and honey

Lunch: Quinoa salad with roasted vegetables and a lemon tahini dressing

Dinner: Stuffed bell peppers with black beans, corn, and salsa

Day 19:

Breakfast: Whole wheat toast with almond butter and sliced bananas

Lunch: Mediterranean-style lentil soup with a side of mixed green salad

Dinner: Vegetable curry with cauliflower rice

Day 20:

Breakfast: Scrambled tofu with spinach and mushrooms, whole grain toast

Lunch: Lentil and vegetable stew with a side of steamed asparagus

Dinner: Stuffed acorn squash with quinoa, cranberries, and walnuts

Day 21:

Breakfast: Greek yogurt with berries and a sprinkle of chopped nuts

Lunch: Caprese salad with fresh mozzarella, tomatoes, and basil

Dinner: Ratatouille served with a side of quinoa pilaf

Day 22:

Breakfast: Oatmeal topped with sliced banana and almonds

Lunch: Chickpea salad with cucumber, cherry tomatoes, and feta cheese

Dinner: Vegetable paella with a side of steamed green beans

Day 23:

Breakfast: Smoothie made with spinach, kale, banana, and almond milk

Lunch: Spinach and ricotta stuffed shells with a side of roasted Brussels sprouts

Dinner: Cauliflower steak with chimichurri sauce and roasted carrots

Day 24:

Breakfast: Avocado toast on whole grain bread with cherry tomatoes

Lunch: Black bean and corn salad with avocado and lime dressing

Dinner: Lentil soup with a side of mixed green salad

Day 25:

Breakfast: Chia seed pudding topped with sliced strawberries

Lunch: Mediterranean quinoa bowl with olives, artichokes, and hummus

Dinner: Vegetable lasagna with a side of steamed broccoli

Day 26:

Breakfast: Whole grain pancakes with blueberry compote

Lunch: Spinach and feta stuffed mushrooms with a side of roasted sweet potatoes

Dinner: Spaghetti squash with marinara sauce and a side of garlic bread

Day 27:

Breakfast: Breakfast burrito with scrambled tofu, black beans, and salsa

Lunch: Roasted vegetable wrap with hummus and arugula

Dinner: Veggie burger on a whole grain bun with roasted cauliflower

Day 28:

Breakfast: Overnight oats with sliced peaches and a drizzle of honey

Lunch: Quinoa tabbouleh with cucumber, tomatoes, and parsley

Dinner: Stuffed portobello mushrooms with a side of roasted root vegetables

Day 29:

Breakfast: Berry smoothie bowl topped with granola and coconut flakes

Lunch: Spinach and strawberry salad with almonds and a balsamic glaze

Dinner: Butternut squash risotto with a side of sautéed spinach

Day 30:

Breakfast: Vegetable Omelet

Lunch: Mediterranean Quinoa Salad

Dinner: Vegetarian Chili

Made in the USA
Coppell, TX
27 February 2025